T0161045

HEARTSTRINGS

POEMS OF
LIFE AND LOVE

KATHRYN CAROLE ELLISON

Published by Lady Bug Books, an imprint of Brisance Books Group.
Lady Bug Press and the distinctive ladybug logo are registered trademarks of
Lady Bug Books, LLC.

Lady Bug Books
400 112th Avenue N.E.
Suite 230
Bellevue, WA 98004
www.ladybugbooks.com

For information about custom editions, special sales and permissions, please contact
Brisance Books Group at specialsales@brisancebooksgroup.com

Manufactured in the United States of America
ISBN: 978-1-944194-05-5

First Edition: April 2016

A NOTE FROM THE AUTHOR

The poems in this book were written over many, many years...
as gifts, of sorts, to my children. I began writing them in the
1970s, when my children were reaching the age of reason and
as I found myself in the position of becoming a single parent.
I needed something special to share with them—something that
would become a tradition, a ritual they could always count on...

And so the Advent Poems began—one day, decades ago—
with a poem 'gifted' to them each day during the December
holiday season every year. The poems were accompanied by a
little trinket or sweet for them to enjoy. Forty years later... my
children still look forward to the poems that started a family
tradition that new generations have come to cherish.
(Or is it the trinkets they love?)

It's my sincere hope that you will embrace and enjoy them
as we have and share them with those you love.

Children of the Light was among the first poems I wrote and
is included in each of my *Poems of Life and Love* books:
Heartstrings, Inspirations, and *Celebrations.* After writing
hundreds of poems, it is still my favorite. The words came
from my heart and my soul and flowed so effortlessly that it
was written in a single sitting. All I needed to do was capture
the words on paper. *Light,* to me, represented all that was
good and pure and right with the world, and I believed then—
as I do today—that those elements live in my children...
and perhaps in all of us. We need only to dare...

DEDICATION

To my parents: Herb and Bernice Haas

Mom, you were the poet who went before me...
unpublished, but appreciated nonetheless.

And Dad, you always believed in me,
no matter what direction my life took.
Thank you for your faith in me,
and for your unconditional love.

TABLE OF CONTENTS

LIFE'S JOYS

LIFE'S LESSONS

LIFE'S GIFTS

LIFE'S JOYS

LISTEN TO YOUR HEART

Sometimes you've tears and you don't know why;
Sometimes you're sad, and your eyes are dry;
Sometimes you feel like dancing...
You're spinning or waltzing or prancing!
You're smiling and laughing and can't seem to stop,
Then all of a sudden you feel a tear drop.

Your feelings are messages from your heart,
Your feelings are what set you apart
From other creatures in our universe.
– whose feelings can be so diverse!
Pay close attention to what's coming through.
The cues and signals are meant for you.

They're where you are and what you need.
They're what to do and how to proceed.
You're the only one to decide your course,
And your feelings do provide a source
Of judgment in making the choices
And listening, carefully, to your heart's voices.

ONE STEP AT A TIME

Little footsteps on the stair
Small-size falters here and there
Progress forward without care.

Midsize footprints on the sand
The journey continues on the land
Occasional need to hold a hand.

Longish strides to the water's edge
Or posed to plunge from off a ledge
To sample all one can of knowledge.

And now to swim, to laugh and shout
To be immersed, to taste, try out
Remain unclosed to all throughout.

Look up, behold! You see the sky
And what must follow is to fly
Sometimes you laugh, sometimes you cry.

The path of life begins so small
When each step taken seems like all
Before you fly you first must crawl.

HAPPINESS

While chasing after a pot of gold
At the end of the rainbow one day,
I met an elf who stopped my trek
And said, "You're going the wrong way!"

"It's in you must go, and deep, my dear.
Your path to treasure lies within."
There lies the only key to happiness there is.
You are the source of origin.

Think of things or people or places
That make you happy and light.
And see them as tiny mirrors that reflect
Your own happy stars burning bright.

In you lies the only key to happiness
That you will ever find.
To get there, go deep into yourself;
Happiness comes from a happy mind.

LIVING LIFE NOW

Don't put off living your life
Until you are feeling strong.
So many people wait.
They've got the plan all wrong.

"I'll do it when I'm older,"
Or, "... when I've learned enough."
"I'll do it when I have more money."
Or, "...find my soul mate." (sob stuff!)

Just do it now, take a bite –
A big bite of life, and then
You won't end up explaining,
"But really, I'll do it when..."

ODE TO ADULTHOOD

We stay forever stuck
In all the psychological muck
About our parent's raising,
Or lack of proper praising.

"She didn't bake me cakes!"
"He didn't like my snakes!"
"She spanked me when she shouldn't!"
"He wanted to hug, but couldn't!"

No matter what our upbringing,
It's woes we're often singing:
"They didn't do it right!"
"My life is just a fright!"

To get past feelings of anguish
We must be willing to relinquish
The past and all its pain,
And get on with our lives again.

Forgiving our parents doesn't mean
We agreed with their whole scene,
Or supported their behavior
As anything superior.

It simply means we're willing
To make our lives fulfilling;
By making the present last,
And letting go of the past.

INSIDE OUT

If all the world has gone awry –
If life is one big alibi –
If things come up that make you cry –
...Just look inside for the answer.

If things go wrong on a daily basis –
If all you see are angry faces –
If people are always on your cases –
...Just look inside for the answer.

It is through our own self–discovery
That our world will make its recovery.
And 'luck' won't seem such a lottery.
...Just look inside for the answer.

CALMNESS

Do people walk away from you feeling calmed?
Do you give off a serene vibration?
Or does the insanity get out of hand,
Leading to nervous agitation?

It's possible for you to stay in control
And not be in total disarray.
If you stay in the calm at the eye of the storm
You're not as likely to get blown away.

You can't help another if you're both unsteady.
The winds of disaster are too strong.
If feathers are ruffled, a gentle stroke
Will help unpleasant matters along.

There's plenty of hysteria in the world –
Too much, at times; so, please, instead
Try to remain calm and hold to your line.
What's needed is at least one level head.

LEAVING THE NEST

The only advice that I can give –
If advice were in order at all –
Is just to be your beautiful selves.
Oh yes, and remember to call.

It occurred to me, quite frankly,
That a parent's job in life
Is to prepare their children to leave the nest
With the confidence to overcome strife.

Your life will have its ups and downs
No matter how well you prepare.
How you handle the changes as they occur
Will have impact on how you'll fare.

The answers will come as you travel your way
Through your life as you pursue
Your careers, your goals and your happiness,
To yourself you must always be true.

Being true to one's self cannot but help
Bring truth and honesty to bear
In dealing with others whom you'll one day meet,
Some for whom you'll have special care.

To care about yourself, of course,
Is your first and foremost goal;
Then caring for others follows naturally;
Honesty and love make you whole.

You are special to me in every way;
I love you just as you are.
I watch and applaud as I see you grow.
Hitch your wagons to a star!

A MOTHER'S WISHES

A positive influence, but not to rule
Is the wish of a mother so fond ..
To have opened a way for you to fly,
To have lovingly allowed a bond.

Instilling confidence so when you're challenged
You know you can succeed,
Instead of doubting and fearing to try
When your little voice says, "No, indeed."

From birth you are taught to trust yourselves
Through another's trust and the absence of fears.
Through trial and error and encouragement
You learn to work through your tears.

Sometimes the wonder of what it's about
Brings nothing specific – a non-answer.
The answers come when the blossom opens,
Or through the movement of the dancer.

My task as mother is simply defined,
And it's a joy to carry out each day:
(It's simply stated, but sometimes difficult to do
– When I get in the way.)

To live within and to live alongside,
To observe and share the trip,
To be your friend and to know your love,
And to firmly let loose the grip.

FRIENDSHIP'S TEST

If you wonder who your friends really are
(...and I don't mean to be dramatic.)
But check to see who is hanging around
When your times are problematic.

When times are good it's easy to say
You've probably many a friend.
But when life gives you a mountain to climb,
Sometimes those friendships end.

But enough about them; how about you?
Are you there for your friend in the swim?
When he's climbing the rungs on his way to success,
Are you holding the ladder for him?

Jealousy never gets you anything
Except too many sleepless nights.
Competition never builds a friendship;
Help each other to reach the heights.

And when your friends are facing a challenge
Be there to extend your hand.
Sometimes an ear is all they need
To know you understand.

CHILDREN OF THE LIGHT

There are those souls who bring the light,
Who spill it out for all to share,
And with a joy that does excite
They show the world that they do care.
It is so very bright.

In this sharing, love does pervade
Into their lives and cycles 'round;
And as this light is outward played
The love is also inward bound.
It is an awesome trade.

You are a soul whose light is shared.
It comes from deep within your heart.
It's best because it is not spared,
Because it's total, not just part.
And I am glad you've dared.

Author's Note:

Of all the poems I have written to and about my children, this one is my favorite.

The Greek Muse Erato was present the evening I put ink to paper to write *Children of the Light* and I shall never forget the feeling of focus and attention as the words spilled out onto the page.

Not a word has been changed in this poem from the night it was written. I believe that my children truly are *Children of the Light*, and everything I am as a mother I owe to them.

It is "an awesome trade."

– KCE

CHOICES

Yes or No, Stay or Go.
Giddyup or Whoa?

Shallow or Deep, Awake or Asleep.
Give Away or Keep?

Present or Past, Finite or Vast.
Dullard or Enthusiast?

Dim or Clear, Front or Rear.
Love or Fear?

LIFE'S LESSONS

FORGIVENESS

We must develop and maintain
The capacity to forgive. Some won't.
It is not always easy to forgive.
Yet, peace eludes us if we don't

There is some good in even the worst of us,
And likewise, some evil in the best.
Awareness of this strange dichotomy
Puts the action of forgiving to the test.

"The weak can never forgive!"
(So said Mahatma Gandhi one day.)
"Forgiveness is an attribute of the strong."
So, forgive without delay.

The wise forgive, but do not forget.
The past is past, without revision.
Forgiveness sets the prisoner free.
That prisoner was you! A good decision!

COURAGE

"Courage is fear that has said its prayers!"
The sentiment rings so loud, so near.
The author's name was somehow lost,
But the message resounds crystal clear.

Our many small journeys often begin
With us in a quaking mental state.
But, trepidation can be dispelled
When on inner strength we concentrate.

Learning to trust ourselves is the key
To gaining the courage that we need.
Just "go inside" and trust you can do it.
Amaze yourself! You will succeed!

EMPATHY

There are two ways of spreading light:
Be the candle or the mirror that reflects it.
The mirror has no opinion about the candle;
It is merely present, to reflect what's been lit.

Empathy is your mirror to reflect;
It mirrors carrying another's burden for awhile.
Empathy is walking in another's shoes
Until they are able to smile.

We underestimate the power of a touch or a smile,
A kind word or a listening ear.
One small act of caring can turn another's life around...
A psychological hug is empathy, my dear.

Self absorption kills empathy, let alone compassion.
Focus on self makes small the world around you.
By focusing on others your world expands.
Your own problems may dim, as you do.

Some people think only intellect counts...
Knowing how to solve problems and get by.
The functions of intellect are insufficient without
Courage, love, friendship, compassion and empathy.

The great gift of humans – we have the power of empathy.
We sense the mysterious connection between souls.
You may not be born with it, but it's a quality you can learn.
Listening is the key, to add true empathy to your goals.

LOVING AND PLEASING

Some words can be used in place of others –
The thesaurus is filled with many.
Once I thought that 'loving' and 'pleasing'
Were as synonymous as any.

Because, I thought, how can you have one
Without the other, too?
If you love someone, wanting always to please
Would be a natural thing to do.

In the end, though, it's more loving to be honest –
With ourselves as well as with our friends.
Honesty allows the energy to flow freely.
Honesty, with love, transcends!

I AM ONLY ONE

These hands, this mind, this willingness
Are all I have to give.
If you but call and ask for help
I'll always be supportive.

I'm only one, but still I'm one,
And there is much that I can do.
I cannot fill your every need,
But then... you don't ask me to.

I will not refuse to be of help
If it's something I can do.
I love the chance to be a part
Of the lives of my dear two.

SOLVING PROBLEMS

The head or the heart, which is the best
For solving the problems of life?
For solving problems you might encounter
With your prospective husband or wife?

The head can do wonders in adding a sum,
Or drawing plans to build a house;
But for solving the differences that may arise,
The head's not the answer with a spouse.

'Every problem we solve with our head creates
Ten more problems,' or so the saying goes.
'While those we solve with our heart stay solved.'
Use your head! Use your heart! Avoid woes!

PEACE

We all want peace; we say the words,
And then wait for peace to come.
But peace eludes our very grasp,
And the struggle seems so wearisome.

Peace is not something to wish for.
It's something you make every day.
It's something you do, and something you are;
And it's something you give away.

LIFE IS A MYSTERY

Life is a mystery, to be sure.
At times we can be insecure.
We strive so that we can procure.
We feel we must at least endure.

A mystery to be lived, it's said
(You wouldn't want to be misled)
Is not a thing for you to dread,
But an adventure – yes! – instead.

You feel that wonders never cease.
In fact, they often do increase.
You learn and grow, gain expertise.
With questions answered, you're at peace.

Do not remain so self–content!
Man wasn't ever really meant
To nod agreement or assent
To 'facts' not so self–evident.

Stay alert! You know the drill.
With practice you will learn the skill
To take in knowledge and distill
Your truth, perhaps, and grow… you will.

Life's not a problem to be solved
Though you, of course, become involved,
In how your mysteries are resolved;
And you, in turn, become evolved.

EXPECTATIONS

Expectations are the worst, by far,
Of all the simple human traps there are.

They tantalize and lull one in to seeing
That people have a constant state of being;

That things remain the same, no matter what;
That attitudes are constant, when they're not.

You must work hard to function in 'today,'
So expectations don't get in the way

Of living life as fully as can be;
And staying in the moment is the key.

By letting go of outcomes from the start,
By loving all who come into one's heart,

Your expectations soon will dissipate,
And free you to fully participate.

DON'T WORRY

Nothing is as hurtful as worry can be;
Nothing's as helpful as concern.
Worry creates even more problems for you.
A fearful, fretting mind cannot learn.

When stumbling blocks such as problems arise,
(They're sure to, if you are in motion...)
Get expert advice; go to someone who knows
About what you have only in 'notion.'

Then look ahead positively from the now and to the future.
Looking back, thinking 'problem and worry'
Merely delays all that is waiting for you
Down the line. That's it! Now, hurry!

Dismiss from your mind each and every disturbance
That cannot be righted by you.
Some things will not change, no matter what's done.
It's a bonus if or when they do.

Assessing realistically, you may see a way
To find that black cloud's silver lining.
You're sure not to find it if you remain in the mode
Of worrying and fretting and whining.

Meet your problems only as they arise.
Each day has enough of its own.
Stay in the now – it's all that we have.
Remain open; let hope set the tone.

EFFORT

The elements cannot do any better than their best:
A star can give only so much light;
A raindrop can give only so much moisture;
And a human so much effort – or might.

Nature functions to its full capacity.
"Should man do any less?" you ask.
The answer is, "No," and of course you realize
That effort makes light work of any task.

You must agree that it is right and proper
To live up to your potential
Then, if that is so, to drop below it
Means you may be missing what's essential.

Nature demands that you live up to your talents,
And make the most of every chance
That presents itself to succeed in life.
What a wonderful thing: your life's dance.

There is only one other thing you can do
After you have done your best.
Angels can do no more than this –
Trust in God for the rest.

A GRATEFUL HEART

A grateful heart is the beginning of greatness.
It is an expression of humility.
It is the foundation of all the virtues,
Like courage, contentment, happiness and nobility.

Humility is not thinking less of yourself.
It is merely thinking of yourself less.
It's not doubting your powers or holding your tongue,
But knowing what's right and acting with thoughtfulness.

Humility is becoming a lost art, it seems.
But it is not difficult to practice each day;
And it begins by realizing that others have been
Involved and helping you along the way.

Maya Angelou said it well: "There are people before me...
I've already been paid for," and {in my wisdom}
I must prepare myself so that I can pay
For someone else who has yet to come.

CREATING BALANCE

Perhaps the single most important challenge
In life is for you to maintain
A balance as you make your way along the path
– A balance that's tricky to obtain.

Between dark and light – between spirit and form...
It's not a choice between extremes.
The challenge is bringing the two together
Into larger themes and precious dreams.

You don't have to choose either conformity or freedom.
Both are appropriate at different times.
And listening to words with acceptance or doubt
Has its place in different paradigms.

It's not one over the other – it's not black or white.
It's seeing what's appropriate when choosing.
It's a balancing act that plays with opposites,
And takes time and thoughtful perusing.

TWO WOLVES

Old Cherokee wisdom passed down to the young
Around a campfire burning bright...
The Elder Woman sharing her stories so wise
To a granddaughter basking in the light.

The subject was about a battle that rages...
(Couched in terms of two wolves in a fight)
The fight goes on inside people each day
Between Good and Evil – wrong and right.

Evil is anger. It's envy and jealousy.
It's sorrow and regret and greed;
On the other hand, Good is joy, peace and love.
It is hope and serenity, truths to heed.

The young girl turned to her grandmother and asked
Her face in an earnest, questioning need...
"Which one wins?" she asked the Elder Woman.
The Old Woman's answer... "The one you feed."

LIFE'S GIFTS

KINDNESS

The basis of kindness is to be consciously
Practicing a most pleasant art –
The art of feeling and seeing yourself
Connected to others, heart to heart.

Kindness itself has two dimensions.
One is vertical; horizontal is the other.
Vertically, we connect deeper with ourselves;
Horizontally, we reach out to another.

No act of kindness is ever wasted,
No matter how small or grand.
Like a boomerang, kindness always returns.
Kindness is perpetually in demand.

True kindness is awareness of others;
It's the currency of our hearts.
As a way of making a difference
It's the most loving of all the arts.

HUMILITY

If no one saw your act of kindness,
Would you do it anyhow?
Do we need a witness to the deed,
Or is doing it enough, somehow?

A humble person does good even though
No one else is there to see.
It's in his nature, he can't be less
Than the best that he – or she – can be.

LOVE OR FEAR

It's love or fear, not both at once;
They don't go hand in hand.
Love should always be the choice.
Read on; you'll understand.

Fear of self is the greatest of terrors,
And the most common of all mistakes.
Failure is sure to follow that fear;
And with your failure, heartaches.

It's said that inaction breeds doubt and fear.
While action breeds confidence and courage.
Go out and get busy – with an open heart.
Reach out; use your talents. Engage!!

And now for a bit of humor, so that
With gloom you're not enveloped:
"Fear is that little darkroom where
Your negatives get developed."

Courage is doing what you are afraid to do.
There's no courage unless you're scared.
It's contagious and affects those around you
To be braver, when you have dared.

Fortune favors the brave, it's said.
Overcome your fear with learning.
There are very few monsters that warrant our fears.
Courage can make you more discerning.

Not being afraid will open your heart.
Look for truth in all you hear.
Remember the title of that now-famous book:
Love Is Letting Go of Fear.

GRATITUDE

Gratitude unlocks the fullness of life.
It turns what we have into more.
It's the healthiest of all the human emotions,
The highest form of thought, and furthermore...

It's the greatest of virtues, the parent of all.
Gratitude helps us to grow and expand.
It brings joy and laughter into our lives.
It makes sense of our past.
We know where we stand.

And as we express our gratitude
We must never forget this wisdom:
The highest appreciation for what we have
Is not to utter the words, but live by them.

DREAMS

Dreams are a glimpse of what can be;
They reach beyond our reality,
Beyond present goals to a wider scope.
They bring new wonder. They bring new hope.

Our dreams are there, an invitation
To dance our own life's interpretation.
The one with which we have been blessed;
The dance we dream of, if confessed.

Without our dreams, what would life be?
Simply stories of emotional bankruptcy!
Without our dreams we'd lose the skill
To look on the other side of the hill.

We must keep dreaming, and never stop!
Dreaming will take us over the top
Of any barrier life could provide.
We reach for our goals with dreams as our guide.

THE MAGIC OF BELIEVING

Believing is a daring adventure for us all.
It's a journey into the unseen.
It's a radiant faith in the yet undiscovered;
It's going where no one has been.

There's magic, my love, in the art of certainty.
"All things are possible to those who believe."
The Master Himself said those words long ago.
Through our consciousness the meaning does weave.

Believe in the limitless supply of God's goodness.
His wonders abound everywhere.
Believe in yourself and your goals in life.
Believe to achieve, and you'll dare.

Believe that you have whatever it takes
And it will be there at your command.
Have faith in others and they'll have faith in you.
Giving and receiving go hand in hand.

'You may be deceived if you trust too much,'
Was the advice of one Frank Crane,
'But you'll live in torment if you don't trust enough.'
You'll lose much less than you gain.

Believe in life's enduring values,
In the good of all mankind.
Stand up and be counted for the things that count.
The peace will still your mind.

Believe that you are quite enough
In order to succeed.
Believe that supply will be at hand
For anything you'll need.

Believe, my love! The magic of believing
Is for you and you alone.
You're the captain of your ship – you stand at the helm
For your own life you set the tone.

CONFIDENCE

If I could give it all to you
I'd give you just one thing.
And that is an image of yourself
That's nothing short of dazzling.

Because with confidence you're in control
Of your actions, and your every thought.
Confidence gives power to everything you do –
Strength for every battle that's fought.

You ask, "How can I be confident
At a time when it just isn't there?
How do I summon what I'm (maybe) not feeling
To meet the demands?" It's not fair!

Confidence comes from positive thinking.
And the opposite, of course, is true.
Know there's a way to meet each demand.
The method is left up to you.

GIVING

"Giving" is an interesting concept.
We think we do it every day –
Our attention, emotion, our material wealth...
Oh yes, we think we pay.

But somewhere in the back of our minds
A voice speaks, and we may recall:
"A gift given with the wrong spirit
Is worse than no gift at all."

When we do something for another,
We must make sure it's for the right reason.
A "want to," not "have to," gift we give
Is good in any season.

And one last thing on the subject of giving
That sums it up in a nutshell:
If loving another is a "job," not a "joy,"
There's more wrong than knowing how to spell.

FREEDOM

Freedom is a personal thing,
An open door that you alone must walk through;
A ladder that you alone must climb
Before it has any true meaning for you.

Though freedom doesn't mean you can do what you please,
It does mean there's nothing to keep
You from pursuing your dreams and your goals
And enjoying all that you reap.

Freedom is an invitation to create
According to your heart's desire;
To respond to that inner urge that you feel,
Working toward that to which you aspire.

Freedom gives you the right to be yourself,
To make mistakes and start anew.
No failure is final, remember that well,
And you'll go far in whatever you do.

A blessing to be shared, freedom allows no conditions
On life or on others you meet.
Freedom comes from within, it's yours to release;
Your future with confidence you'll greet.

YOUR UNIQUE GIFT

Each of us is blessed with a gift.
As we journey through life it becomes known.
Your gift is worth nothing till you give it away.
Watch the seeds grow as they're sown.

In the eyes of the world your gift may be small,
Or larger than any gift going.
But it matters not the size or scope.
What matters is your love outflowing.

It is through the finding and the giving
Of this gift with which you're blessed
That you find the joy that's at the core
Of being and doing your best.

Identify one talent that you possess
That has enriched the life of another.
Rejoice in your ability to joyfully give.
It's unlike any other.

WORDS

A word, once spoken, cannot be called back.
It has the power to be hurtful or kind.
To use words wisely takes a special knack...
One that is, at times, hard to find.

The wounds from some words can be hard to mend;
Social intercourse, at best, is tough.
Thoughtless comments are hard to defend.
Learn to know when you have said enough.

YOU LIVE IN MY HEART

You're away from home, and yet so near;
You live here in my heart.
You're on your own, you're all grown up,
Yet we'll never be apart.

I've given you all that I can give,
In terms of parenting things.
In all ways now, you make your path;
You are free to spread your wings.

I have total faith that you'll excel
In all that you attempt.
Just keep your minds open and positive,
Hold no one in contempt.

We're complex, it's true, my dears. We are.
We aren't made up of just one thing.
I like to think we're three parts in all,
Held together by a magic string.

In terms of health it takes all three
To keep you well and growing...
Your physical part, and mental, too,
And the spiritual part for glowing.

Be the very best that you can be;
Do the best that you can do
Each day, my loves; one day at a time.
Your light comes shining through.

I love you so, I hope you know
That even when we're apart
Our love is pure, our love is true.
You are precious in my heart.

REMEMBER ME

When you remember me it means
That I have left some mark
Of who I am on who you are.
Between us there's a spark.

It means you've carried part of me
Within your mind or heart.
It means I can be summoned back,
Though years or miles apart.

It means that if we meet again
You'll know just who I am.
After I die, you'll see my face,
And heartspeak... to the hologram.

For as long as you remember me
I'm not entirely gone.
When I'm feeling my most ghostlike,
Your remembering carries me on.

A CLOSING THOUGHT

POETRY

It's the revelation
Of a sensation
That the poet
(Wouldn't you know it)
Believes to be
Felt only interiorly
And personal to
The writer who
… **writes it.**

It's the interpretation
Of a sensation
That was fueled by
A poet's sigh
And believed to be
Shared mutually
And personal to
The lucky one who
… **reads it.**

About the author

Kathryn Carole Ellison is a former newspaper columnist
and journalist and, of course, a poet.

She lives near her children and stepchildren and their families in the
Pacific Northwest, and spends winters in the sunshine of Arizona.

You might find her on the golf course with friends, river rafting,
writing poems... or at the opera.

Late bloomer

Our culture honors youth with all
It's unbridled effervescence.
We older ones sit back and nod
As if in acquiescence.

And when our confidence really gels
In early convalescence...
'We can't be getting old!' we cry,
'We're still struggling with adolescence!'

Acknowledgments

I have many people to thank...

First of all, my children Jon and Nicole LaFollette, for
inspiring the writing of these poems in the first place.
And for encouraging me to continue my writing, even
though their wisdom and compassion surpass mine.

My wonderful stepchildren, Debbie and John Bacon,
Jeff and Sandy Ellison, and Tom and Sue Ellison, who,
with their children and grandchildren, continue to be a
major part of my life and are loved deeply by me.
These poems are for you, too.

Eva LaFollette, the dearest daughter-in-law one could
ever wish for... and one of my dearest friends.
Your encouragement and interest are so appreciated.

My good friends who have received a poem or two
of mine in their Christmas cards these many years, for
complimenting me on the messages in my poems.
Your encouragement kept me writing.

To Kim Kiyosaki who introduced me to the right person
to get the publishing process underway... that person
being Mona Gambetta with Brisance Books Group
who has the experience and know-how to make
these books happen.

And finally, to John Laughlin, a fellow traveler in life, who
encourages me every day in the writing and publishing
process. John, I love having you in my cheering section!

OTHER BOOKS

by Kathryn Carole Ellison

CELEBRATIONS

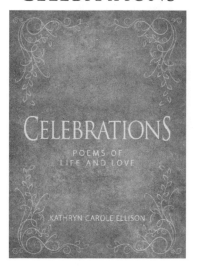

INSPIRATIONS

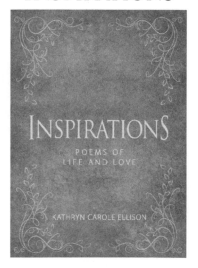